THROW AN INDEPENDENCE DAY PARTY

BY ELIZABETH NEUENFELDT

Express!

BELLWETHER MEDIA • MINNEAP

Express!

Imagination comes alive in **Express!**
Transform the everyday into the fresh and new, discover ways to stir up flavor and excitement, and experiment with new ideas and materials. Express! makerspace books: where your next creative adventure begins!

This edition first published in 2023 by Bellwether Media, Inc.

No part of this publication may be reproduced in whole or in part without written permission of the publisher. For information regarding permission, write to Bellwether Media, Inc., Attention: Permissions Department, 6012 Blue Circle Drive, Minnetonka, MN 55343.

Library of Congress Cataloging-in-Publication Data

Names: Neuenfeldt, Elizabeth, author.
Title: Throw an Independence Day party / by Elizabeth Neuenfeldt.
Description: Minneapolis, MN : Bellwether Media, Inc., 2023. | Series: Express!: Party time! | Includes bibliographical references and index. | Audience: Ages 7-13 | Audience: Grades 4-6 | Summary: "Information accompanies step-by-step instructions for various crafts and recipes for an Independence Day Party. The text level and subject matter are intended for students in grades 3 through 8"-- Provided by publisher.
Identifiers: LCCN 2022047986 (print) | LCCN 2022047987 (ebook) | ISBN 9798886871876 (library binding) | ISBN 9798886873139 (ebook)
Subjects: LCSH: Fourth of July decorations--Juvenile literature. | Fourth of July celebrations--Juvenile literature. | Children's parties--Juvenile literature.
Classification: LCC TT900.F68 N48 2023 (print) | LCC TT900.F68 (ebook) | DDC 745.594/1--dc23/eng/20221013
LC record available at https://lccn.loc.gov/2022047986
LC ebook record available at https://lccn.loc.gov/2022047987

Editor: Christina Leaf   Series Design: Jeffrey Kollock   Book Designer: Laura Sowers
Projects and Project Photography: Jessica Moon   Craft Instructions: Sarah Eason

Printed in the United States of America, North Mankato, MN.

TABLE OF CONTENTS

THROW AN INDEPENDENCE DAY PARTY!

Independence Day happens in the United States each year on July 4. This day honors the **founding fathers** approving the **Declaration of Independence** on July 4, 1776. It also honors how the 13 American **colonies** won against **Great Britain** in the **Revolutionary War**.

You can honor Independence Day with friends and family by throwing a party. This book will help you fill your gathering with shiny stars, festive stripes, and more. From party hats and paper chain decorations to delicious food and drinks, there are many projects to try out! Get ready to throw your own **patriotic** party!

TOP TIP

Look for this feature throughout the book. It will give you tips to help improve your projects.

MATERIALS AND TOOLS

To make your party projects, you will need some basic art supplies, such as colored cardstock and paper. You will also need some basic kitchen tools, including knives, forks, spoons, cutting boards, and mixing and serving bowls.

You will also need:
- glue
- scissors
- pencils
- markers
- paints
- paintbrushes
- tape

CELEBRATION PARTY HATS

Extra materials needed:
red, white, and blue
   glitter cardstock
1 large sheet of blue paper
3 paper straws
stapler

Stars are a popular **symbol** of Independence Day. The American flag is covered in 50 white stars to represent the country's 50 states. The first American flag had 13 stars. More stars were added as the country grew. Since 1777, there have been 27 different flags. In this craft, you will cut out stars to create festive party hats. Try one on!

1
From your glitter cardstock, cut out a large star in each color.

2
Cut out a medium-sized star in each color. Glue them onto the center of the large stars, as shown below.

3
Cut out a small star in each color. Glue them onto the center of the medium stars, as shown below.

4

Cut a length of blue paper tall enough to make a hat. Wrap it around your head and mark where the ends meet. Cut off any excess paper, then glue or staple the ends together.

5

Now, glue the stars you made in Step 3 onto the front of your hat.

TOP TIP

To make your stars extra secure, use a piece of tape to hold them in place.

6

Repeat Steps 1 through 3, alternating the colors differently from last time. Glue the final stars onto your paper straws. Once dry, tape the straws to the inside of your hat to complete it. Repeat the activity so that there are enough party hats for all of the guests.

FINAL

PATRIOTIC PAPER CHAIN

Extra materials needed:
4 sheets of red, white, and blue paper
stapler
silver marker

Red and white stripes are found on many Fourth of July decorations. They are an important part of the American flag. The flag has thirteen stripes. Seven stripes are red. Six stripes are white. Altogether, they represent the 13 colonies that fought in the Revolutionary War. Celebrate the flag and its symbolism with this patriotic paper chain!

1

Start with a piece of red paper. Cut the paper into four strips lengthwise.

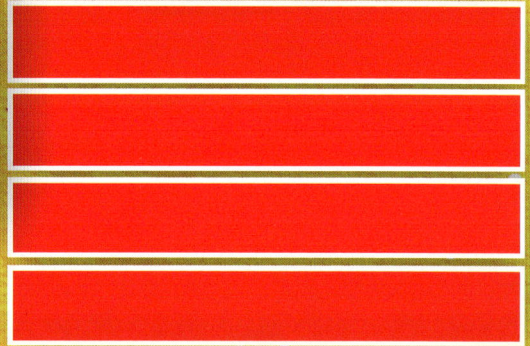

2

Take some white paper and cut it into eight 0.5-inch (1-centimeter) strips. Glue two white strips onto each of the red strips of paper you created in Step 1. Let dry.

3

Cut a piece of blue paper into four strips lengthwise. Draw several silver stars onto the center of each strip.

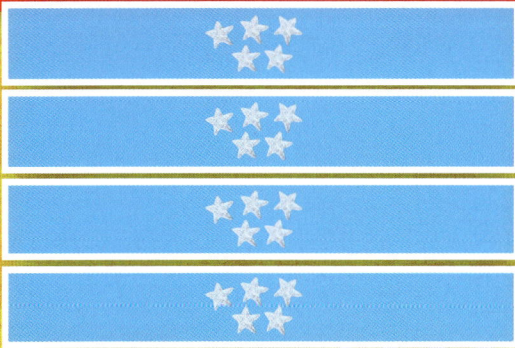

4

Roll a blue strip into a band and staple together, as shown.

staple

5

Thread a red and white strip of paper through the blue band, as shown. Staple the ends of the red and white band together. Thread another blue band through the red and white band and staple together. Repeat until all of your strips have been used.

staple

TOP TIP

To make longer paper chains, create more strips of paper and attach them to the first paper chain.

FINAL

VEGGIE DIP FLAG

Extra materials needed:

serving tray or board
square dish
vegetable peeler
garlic dip
blue food coloring
cherry tomatoes
celery sticks
red pepper
cucumber

Betsy Ross is famous for making the first American flag in 1777. But while Betsy sewed many American flags, there is no proof she made the first one. Some historians think founding father Francis Hopkinson designed the flag. No matter who made the first one, you can make your own tasty American flag with vegetables and dip!

SAFETY TIP

Have an adult help you safely use the knife and vegetable peeler.

1

Place your tray or board on your work surface. Place the square dish in the top left corner, as shown.

2

Take your dip and add a few drops of blue food coloring. Mix well, then pour it into your square dish.

10

3

Cut your tomatoes in half, then place about one-third of them along the top edge of the tray.

4

Slice your celery into thin strips, then place about one-third of the strips below the tomatoes.

5

Slice your red pepper into thin strips, then place about one-third of the strips beneath the celery.

TURN THE PAGE! ▶

TOP TIP

You can swap one vegetable for another of the same color if you prefer.

6

Peel and slice your cucumber, then place about one-third of the slices beneath the pepper.

7

Place the rest of your tomatoes in a long line beneath the dip dish and the cucumber.

8

Place the rest of your celery beneath your tomatoes.

9

Place the rest of your red pepper beneath your celery.

10

Place the rest of your cucumber beneath your peppers. Your veggie dip flag is now ready to serve!

FINAL

TOP TIP

To make a sweet version of this snack, swap the vegetables for fruit and serve it with a yogurt dip instead.

13

FREEDOM FRUIT PIZZA

Extra materials needed:

sheet of ready-made
  cookie dough
baking tray
oven mitts
whipped cream
1 package of blueberries
1 package of raspberries

Many Americans celebrate Independence Day with red, white, and blue foods. They do this to honor the colors of the American flag. Each color of the flag has a special meaning. Red symbolizes bravery, white represents **innocence**, and blue stands for **justice**. For this recipe, you will use raspberries, blueberries, and whipped cream to make your own patriotic treat!

SAFETY TIP

Ask an adult to help bake the dough. Make sure they use oven mitts, too!

1

Spread your sheet of cookie dough on a board. Put a large plate on top of the dough and cut around it to make a circle. Place it on a baking tray, then bake following the packet instructions. When fully baked, remove and leave to cool on a plate. This will be your fruity pizza base.

2

Once the base is cool, cover it with whipped cream.

3

Place some of your blueberries in the top left corner of your pizza.

4

Add your raspberries in rows, making sure you leave a gap between each row.

5

Finish by adding your remaining blueberries around the edge.

FINAL

STARS AND STRIPES DRINK

Many families enjoy ice cream to stay cool on the Fourth of July. This frozen treat was also a favorite among some of the founding fathers. Thomas Jefferson, the third U.S. president, even had his own ice cream recipe! For this activity, you will use ice cream to make your own festive drink. One recipe should make two drinks. Yum!

1 Place the frozen berries and a large scoop of ice cream into your blender cup.

2 Add a little milk at a time, then blend until the mixture becomes a thick shake.

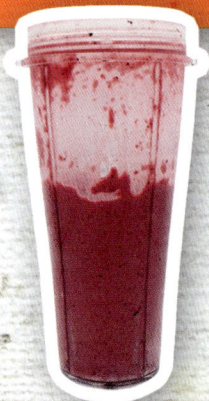

3 Pour half of the mixture into a glass, then place in the fridge to chill.

16

4 Meanwhile, place three scoops of ice cream in your blender cup. Add a cup of milk and a teaspoon of blue food coloring.

5 Blend until the mixture forms a shake. It will be thinner than the first berry shake.

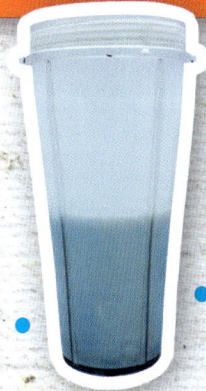

7 Top with whipped cream and a sprinkling of star-shaped sprinkles.

6 Gently pour the blue shake over the red shake in the glass. Take care not to disturb the red layer.

FINAL

BALLOON POP PARTY GAME

Fireworks are a highlight of many Independence Day celebrations. These loud, colorful explosions have been used to celebrate Independence Day since 1777! This patriotic game recreates the loud pops of fireworks. Players take turns throwing three darts to pop balloons. They keep score of the number of balloons they pop. Whoever pops the most balloons is the winner!

1

Take your cardboard box, flatten it, and cut it into a rectangle.

2

Paint the cardboard white and let it dry.

3

Once the cardboard is dry, blow up 12 blue balloons. Tape them in three lines to the top left corner of the cardboard.

4

Blow up five red balloons and tape them in a line across the top of the cardboard, starting to the right of the blue balloons.

TURN THE PAGE! ▶

5

Blow up five white balloons and tape them in a line beneath the red balloons.

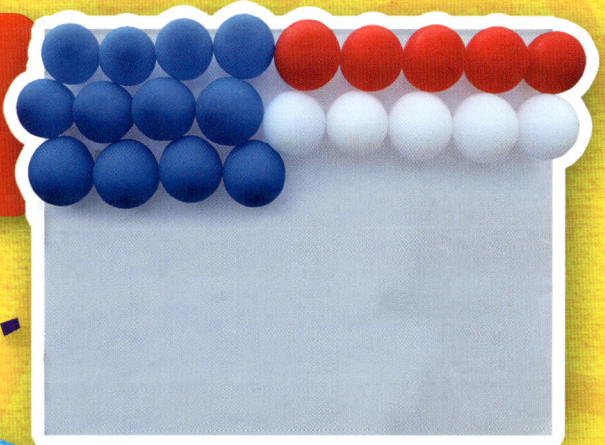

Blow up another five red balloons and tape them in a line beneath the white balloons.

Blow up nine white balloons and tape them in a line beneath the blue and red balloons.

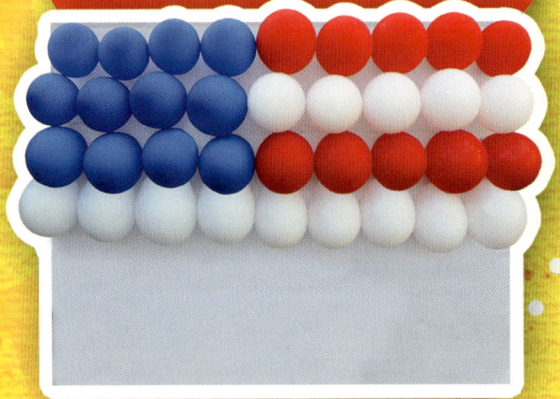

Blow up nine red balloons and tape them in a line beneath the white balloons.

Blow up nine white balloons and tape them in a line beneath the red balloons.

10

Blow up nine red balloons and tape them in a line beneath the white balloons. Finally, cut out six stars from your silver cardstock and attach them to alternate blue balloons to finish your pop flag.

Use the flag as a decoration until you are ready to play your balloon pop game!

FINAL

GLOSSARY

colonies—areas controlled by another country

Declaration of Independence—a document that was approved on July 4, 1776, that stated the 13 American colonies were free from British rule

founding fathers—the men who helped the 13 colonies in America to become a country

Great Britain—an island in western Europe that is made up of present-day England, Scotland, and Wales; Great Britain is now part of the United Kingdom.

innocence—the state of being free from guilt

justice—fair treatment

patriotic—showing love for one's country

Revolutionary War—the war from 1775 to 1783 in which the United States fought for independence from Britain

symbol—something that stands for something else

TO LEARN MORE

AT THE LIBRARY

Gagne, Tammy. *Fact and Fiction of the American Revolution.* Minneapolis, Minn.: Abdo Publishing, 2022.

Miles, David. *The Side-by-side Declaration of Independence: With Side-by-side "Plain English" Translations, Plus Definitions, and More!* Fresno, Calif.: Bushel & Peck Books, 2021.

Murray, Stuart. *American Revolution.* New York, N.Y.: DK Publishing, 2022.

ON THE WEB

FACTSURFER

Factsurfer.com gives you a safe, fun way to find more information.

1. Go to www.factsurfer.com.

2. Enter "Independence Day party" into the search box and click 🔍.

3. Select your book cover to see a list of related content.

INDEX

All photos in this book are provided through the courtesy of Calcium.